COMPLEX PTSD

Your Practical Guide for Complete Healing from Trauma and Toxic Relationships

Laura Gardner

Table of Contents

Laura Gardner

Before you start reading this book, I want to offer you a free e-book – How to Say No Without Feeling Guilty. Scan this QR code or click here to claim your free e-book now!

Introduction

The Whole Person Approach

If you're reading this, you've definitely been through a lot. Life may have thrown more at you than anyone should have to endure, and yet, here you are—seeking to understand, to heal, and to move forward. Let me start by saying, I'm really glad you're here.

Complex PTSD, or C-PTSD, isn't something we hear about as much as regular PTSD, but for many of us, it's the term that fits our experiences more accurately. PTSD usually refers to a single traumatic event, like a car accident or a natural disaster. Complex PTSD, though, happens when we've experienced prolonged, repeated trauma— often at the hands of those we trusted. It's like experiencing one isolated storm versus enduring an unending hurricane.

I know what that feels like. I've worked with people who have survived childhood abuse, domestic violence, and emotional neglect, and I've seen firsthand how deeply these experiences shape us. But I've also seen people break free. I've watched them heal, step by step, and I've been privileged to walk alongside them in that process. That's why I'm writing this book: to walk alongside you, too.

What Is Complex PTSD?

Complex PTSD often feels like living with your trauma every day. It can show up in ways that make you doubt yourself, struggle with relationships, or even feel like you're broken beyond repair. But here's what I want you to know from the very start: You are not broken. The very fact that you've survived what you have is a testament to your strength, even if it doesn't always feel that way.

Our bodies and brains are wired to protect us, and sometimes they do this by holding onto trauma. It's why certain things may trigger you out of nowhere, or why you might feel overwhelmed when you think you should be fine. These reactions aren't your fault—they're your system's way of keeping you safe, even if that system now feels like it's working against you.

I remember working with a client who found it difficult to feel comfortable in her own body. Whenever we'd start talking about her experiences, she'd go stiff, her breath would quicken, and she'd want to shut down the conversation completely. It wasn't that she didn't want to heal, it was that her body was protecting her the only way it knew how: by dissociating. Her experience taught me that healing from Complex PTSD isn't just about talking through what happened. It involves engaging with your entire being—your thoughts, body, and feelings.

A Whole-Person Approach

That's why this book is all about a whole-person approach. You might have already tried therapy (maybe more than once), and that's great. But healing from Complex PTSD requires more than just one tool—it requires integrating multiple approaches that address every part of you that's been affected by trauma. This includes your nervous system, your thought patterns, and the way you relate to yourself and others.

We're going to explore methods like mindfulness, which helps you reconnect with the present moment without being hijacked by the past. I'll also introduce you to somatic psychology, which is all about listening to your body and gently releasing the trauma it's been holding. You'll learn practical tools from Cognitive Behavioral Therapy (CBT) to reframe negative thought patterns, and I'll guide you through the fascinating world of EMDR (Eye Movement Desensitization and Reprocessing)—a therapy that has transformed the lives of many trauma survivors.

We'll also go into the deeper, more personal work of parts therapy. This is where you'll get to know the different parts of yourself—the wounded parts that are still trying to protect you and the parts that want to heal. I know this might sound a bit "out there" at first, but trust me, it's powerful work.

Why Self-Compassion Matters

One of the hardest things about Complex PTSD is how it warps our relationship with ourselves. You might feel angry at yourself for not being able to "just move on," or maybe you blame yourself for things that were never your fault to begin with. But healing isn't about pushing yourself harder. It involves practicing the same kindness and understanding towards yourself that you would extend to a dear friend.

In fact, let me share something personal. Years ago, I struggled with the idea of self-compassion. I thought it was too "soft," and that if I wasn't hard on myself, I'd never get better. But I was wrong. It wasn't until I learned to be kind to myself—to speak to myself with patience and understanding—that real healing started to happen. That's when it became clear to me that self-compassion is not a luxury but a fundamental need. And it's something I hope to help you cultivate as we go through this book.

What to Expect

Throughout this book, you'll find practical exercises, tools, and techniques designed to support your healing process. You don't have to do everything at once—in fact, I encourage you to go at your own pace. Some chapters might feel tough to get through, and that's okay. Take breaks when you need to. Healing from Complex PTSD isn't a race; it's a journey that requires patience and, yes, self-compassion. By the end of this book, I hope you'll feel more connected to your body, more compassionate towards yourself, and more empowered to take control of your healing.

You've already taken a huge step by picking up this book. The journey is challenging, but you don't need to face it by yourself. I'm here with you, and together, we're going to see what it means to heal—one step at a time.

PART 1: THE FOUNDATIONS OF HEALING FROM COMPLEX PTSD

Chapter 1

The Body Keeps the Score

Trauma is not a mere event that occurs and then disappears over time. It doesn't vanish once the cause is over. Instead, it stays with you, living in your body in ways that can be hard to understand—until you start paying attention to the signs. Your body is like a memory keeper, holding onto the effects of prolonged trauma even when your mind wants to forget.

I remember the first time I truly understood this concept. A client of mine would come into sessions feeling exhausted, tense, and sometimes even in physical pain. She couldn't connect her body's symptoms to her traumatic experiences, though. It was as if her body was speaking a language she didn't know how to translate. But as we worked together, she began to realize something many trauma survivors eventually discover: her body had been trying to protect her all along, storing the pain, fear, and stress she couldn't process at the time.

How Trauma Lives in the Body

So, how exactly does trauma live in the body?

When we experience a traumatic event, our bodies go into survival mode, activating the stress response system that's been with us since humans roamed the wild. This system is designed to protect us from danger, flooding the body with hormones like cortisol and adrenaline to prepare us to either fight, flee, or freeze. In the short term, this response is incredibly useful. If you're facing immediate danger, like a predator (or, more realistically, a dangerous person), your body's natural reaction gives you the energy and focus you need to get through it.

But when the trauma is ongoing—whether it's childhood neglect, domestic abuse, or chronic emotional manipulation—your body never gets a chance to relax. It remains on high alert, and over time, this constant state of vigilance takes a toll. Your nervous system becomes dysregulated, and your body stores the trauma in your muscles, organs, and cells. It's why many survivors of complex trauma experience chronic pain, tension, or a sense of being disconnected from their bodies.

In my client's case, she developed tightness in her shoulders and neck that wouldn't go away, no matter how many massages or physical therapy sessions she tried. That tightness was her body's way of saying, "We've been in survival mode for a long time, and we haven't yet learned how to feel safe again."

This is a reality for so many people dealing with Complex PTSD. It's not just a mental or emotional battle—it's physical too. Trauma impacts how we move, breathe, and feel inside our own skin.

How the Brain Reacts to Prolonged Trauma: Fight, Flight, Freeze, and Fawn Responses

When we think of trauma responses, most people know about the famous trio: fight, flight, and freeze. But there's another response that often gets overlooked: the fawn response. Let's break them down, so you can start identifying how your body might be reacting to trauma, even long after the danger has passed.

Fight Response

The fight response is pretty straightforward—your body prepares to face the threat head-on. You might feel anger or aggression, your heart rate increases, and your muscles tense up. While this can be a powerful and effective survival strategy, prolonged trauma can leave you in a constant state of irritability or defensiveness, even when there's no immediate threat.

Flight Response

When we talk about the flight response, think of it as your body telling you to get out, fast. You might feel an urge to run, avoid, or escape a situation. People with a strong flight response might experience constant restlessness, anxiety, or the need to stay busy, as though still trying to outrun the trauma. For some, this can turn into chronic anxiety, always anticipating danger even when they're physically safe.

Freeze Response

The freeze response is when your body shuts down. In the wild, animals freeze to avoid detection by predators, and humans have inherited this survival tactic. You might feel numb, detached, or dissociate entirely. When I worked with Sarah, she would often describe feeling "frozen" during arguments with her abusive partner—like she couldn't move, couldn't speak, and couldn't protect herself, even when she wanted to. Over time, freeze responses can make you feel disconnected from your body and emotions, almost as though you're watching your life happen from the outside.

Fawn Response

The fawn response is one we don't hear about as much, but it's incredibly common among trauma survivors, especially those who experienced abuse or neglect. When you "fawn," your

body's survival instinct is to please or appease the person threatening you. This might look like excessive people-pleasing, avoiding conflict at all costs, or prioritizing the needs of others over your own. For many, this response develops in childhood, when the only way to stay safe is to keep the adults around you happy.

Over time, these survival responses become ingrained in your nervous system, shaping how you react to stress, conflict, or even everyday situations. You might not even realize when your body is going into fight, flight, freeze, or fawn mode, but understanding these reactions is key to healing.

The Mind-Body Connection in Healing Trauma

So, what do we do with all this knowledge? If trauma lives in the body, then healing must happen in the body too. And this is where the mind-body connection becomes so important. You can't think your way out of trauma—you have to feel your way through it.

That might sound like torture, but it doesn't have to be. Healing the body isn't about diving headfirst into painful memories or forcing yourself to relive trauma. It's about slowly, gently reconnecting with yourself in a way that feels safe and supportive.

When I first started exploring somatic (body-based) therapy with clients, I was amazed by how transformative it could be. I remember one client who struggled with panic attacks for years. She had tried cognitive approaches, like CBT, and while they helped her understand her triggers, they didn't stop her body from reacting as though it was still in danger. But once we started integrating body awareness into our sessions—focusing on her breath, gently stretching, and noticing sensations in her body—her panic attacks began to decrease. She learned to calm her nervous system not just through thought, but through movement and presence.

Breath and Movement

Breathwork and movement are two incredibly powerful tools for healing trauma in the body. When we're in survival mode, our breathing becomes shallow and fast, which signals to the brain that we're in danger. Learning to breathe deeply—especially when we feel triggered—can help calm the nervous system and bring us back to the present moment.

In the same way, movement can help release tension stored in the body. This doesn't have to be intense exercise (though that works for some people); it can be as simple as gentle stretching or walking. The key is to reconnect with your body in a way that feels good to you.

Mindfulness and Body Awareness

Mindfulness is another tool I use regularly with clients. It's about tuning into the present moment without judgment, allowing yourself to notice sensations, thoughts, and feelings without trying to change them. When applied to trauma healing, mindfulness can help you start to feel safe in your body again. It's about learning to notice the signals your body is sending and responding to them with curiosity instead of fear.

Self-Compassion

And finally, we can't talk about the mind-body connection without talking about self-compassion. When your body feels like an enemy or a stranger, it's hard to extend kindness to yourself, but self-compassion is essential for healing. It's about recognizing that your body has been doing its best to protect you all this time, even if those protections now feel like barriers.

When this client and I worked together, one of the biggest shifts happened when she started to see her body not as something that had betrayed her, but as a part of her that had been trying, in its own way, to keep her safe. Once she embraced this idea, she began to approach her healing with more patience and care.

Recognizing how trauma dwells in your body is the first step towards taking back control of your life. Throughout this book, we're going to discuss different ways to reconnect with yourself, calm your nervous system, and release the trauma that's been held inside for so long.

Remember, healing is a process. You don't have to fix everything right now, and you certainly don't have to do it alone. But by understanding the mind-body connection, you're giving yourself the tools to start feeling whole again.

Chapter 2

Mindful Awareness: First Steps in Healing

When I first discovered mindfulness, I was skeptical. How could something as simple as paying attention to your breath or noticing the sounds around you help heal the deep, complex wounds left by trauma? But the more I explored it for myself and with clients, the more I realized that mindfulness wasn't just a tool for stress relief or relaxation—it was an essential piece of the puzzle for reconnecting with the body, calming the mind, and beginning the long process of healing.

Trauma, especially the kind we're talking about with Complex PTSD, disconnects us from ourselves. It pulls us into survival mode, where we're so focused on just getting through the day that we lose touch with how we feel, what we need, and what's happening inside us. Mindfulness is one of the first steps toward healing because it gently invites us to come back into our bodies, to notice what's happening in the present moment, and to begin the slow, careful process of feeling safe again.

Mindfulness and Its Role in Trauma Recovery

At its core, mindfulness is about awareness—specifically, being aware of the present moment without judgment. It's about paying attention to what is happening *right now*, whether it's your breath, the way your body feels, or the thoughts running through your mind. And while that might sound simple, the impact mindfulness can have on trauma recovery is profound.

Why? Because trauma lives in the past. When you've experienced prolonged trauma, your body and mind are constantly bracing for the next danger, often replaying old hurts or anticipating future ones. You become stuck in a loop of fear, hypervigilance, and anxiety, always preparing for the worst. Mindfulness helps break that loop by grounding you in the present.

When you practice mindfulness, you're not denying or pushing away your trauma. Instead, you're gently shifting your focus to what's happening in the here and now. This simple act of bringing your attention to the present moment helps calm the nervous system and reduces the constant state of fight, flight, freeze, or fawn that so many trauma survivors experience.

I've seen this shift firsthand in my work with clients. One in particular, a man who had survived years of childhood abuse, used to describe his mind as a "whirlwind of fear." He was constantly reliving the worst moments of his past, unable to shake the feeling that something terrible was about to happen again. When we first started practicing mindfulness, it was hard for him to stay in the present even for a minute. But over time, he began to notice the small moments of peace that mindfulness brought. Those moments stretched longer and longer until he could finally say that the "whirlwind" wasn't controlling him anymore.

Mindfulness doesn't erase trauma, but it gives you a tool to stop it from running your life.

Mindfulness Exercises to Begin Reconnecting with Your Body

If you're new to mindfulness, it can feel intimidating at first. Sitting still and paying attention to your breath might seem like the last thing you want to do, especially if you're someone who's used to staying busy to avoid feeling the weight of your emotions. But mindfulness doesn't have to be complicated or overwhelming. It's about small, simple moments of awareness.

Let's start with a few basic exercises. You don't need any special equipment or a quiet meditation room to do these—just a willingness to show up for yourself, wherever you are.

1. Mindful Breathing

Mindful breathing is one of the easiest and most effective ways to start reconnecting with your body. You're breathing all the time, so why not make it an anchor to the present moment?

Here's how to begin:

- Find a comfortable seat or lie down, whatever feels best for you.

- Close your eyes if you feel safe doing so, or soften your gaze by looking at a spot on the floor.

- Take a slow, deep breath through your nose, feeling your chest and belly expand.

- Slowly exhale through your mouth, letting your body relax with each out-breath.

- As you breathe, gently focus on the sensation of the air entering and leaving your body.

- If your mind starts to wander (which it will—this is normal!), simply notice where it went and gently bring your attention back to your breath.

Start with just a few minutes a day and gradually increase the time as you feel more comfortable. This simple practice helps ground you in the present moment and brings awareness to the sensations in your body, which is key in trauma recovery.

2. Body Scan

A body scan is another way to reconnect with your body by bringing mindful attention to each part of it, one at a time. This practice helps you notice where you might be holding tension, discomfort, or emotion in your body—things you may not even realize are there.

To try a body scan:

- Sit or lie down in a comfortable position.

- Close your eyes and take a few deep breaths to settle in.

- Starting at the top of your head, slowly bring your attention to each part of your body, moving downward. Notice the sensations (or lack of sensations) in your scalp, forehead, temples, eyes, and jaw. Is there tension? Relaxation? Neutrality?

- Move down to your neck, shoulders, and arms, noticing any sensations or areas that feel tight or sore.

- Continue down your torso, legs, and feet, simply observing what you feel without judgment.

- If you notice tension or discomfort, imagine breathing into that part of your body and letting it soften with each exhale.

The body scan is a great way to bring awareness to your physical body and start noticing how trauma might be manifesting there. With time, it can also help you build a sense of safety and connection with your body.

3. Five Senses Grounding Exercise

Grounding exercises like this one are particularly helpful when you feel anxious, overwhelmed, or disconnected. This exercise anchors you to the present moment by using your five senses.

Here's how to do it:

- Take a deep breath and look around you.

- Name *five things* you can see.

- Name *four things* you can touch.

- Name *three things* you can hear.

- Name *two things* you can smell.

- Name *one thing* you can taste.

This quick exercise helps pull you out of your mind and back into your body. It's also a great way to calm down when you're feeling triggered or anxious.

Benefits of Mindfulness

Mindfulness isn't just about feeling "zen" or relaxed. It's a powerful tool for grounding yourself and regulating your emotions, especially when dealing with the aftermath of trauma.

1. Grounding

When you've experienced prolonged trauma, it's easy to get caught up in the past or future. You might find yourself replaying traumatic memories, worrying about what's going to happen next, or feeling like you're stuck in survival mode. Mindfulness helps break that cycle by grounding you in the present.

Grounding techniques like mindful breathing or the five senses exercise help you connect to what's happening right now, rather than getting lost in the "what ifs" or "what was." Over time, grounding through mindfulness can create a sense of safety in your body, which is essential for healing.

2. Emotional Regulation

Trauma can make it feel like your emotions are out of control, swinging from numbness to overwhelming fear, anger, or sadness. Mindfulness helps by creating a space between the emotion and your reaction to it. Instead of being swept away by an emotion, you can observe it, acknowledge it, and respond in a way that feels less reactive.

For example, let's say you notice yourself getting angry. Instead of lashing out or shutting down, mindfulness teaches you to pause and observe that anger—where do you feel it in your body? What thoughts are fueling it? By staying with the emotion, rather than running from it, you begin to understand it more clearly and respond to it with more intention.

3. Building Self-Awareness

Mindfulness is also a way of building self-awareness, which is key to healing from trauma. It helps you tune into your body's signals and recognize patterns of thought, emotion, and behavior that might not be serving you. As you become more aware, you can make more conscious choices about how to respond to triggers or difficult emotions.

Mindfulness is a gentle but powerful tool for trauma recovery. It's not about forcing yourself to feel better or "fixing" anything—it's about being present with yourself, as you are, and slowly rebuilding the connection between your mind and body. The more you practice, the more you'll find that mindfulness gives you space to heal, breathe, and reclaim your life from trauma.

Chapter 3

Self-Compassion: The Key to Healing

If there's one thing I wish I could tell everyone recovering from trauma, it's this: Be kind to yourself. It sounds simple, doesn't it? But I know, from both personal experience and working with others, that self-compassion is one of the hardest things to embrace when you've been through the depths of Complex PTSD. We are often our own harshest critics, especially when we've survived prolonged trauma. The inner voice can be brutal—constantly reminding us of what we should've done differently, why we weren't strong enough, why we feel so broken. And yet, this harshness only deepens the wounds.

Self-compassion is the antidote to that voice. It's about showing yourself the same kindness you would offer a dear friend who's struggling. It's about learning to treat yourself with care, understanding, and patience as you navigate the difficult journey of healing.

For many of us, this feels foreign. We've spent years blaming ourselves for what happened, thinking we were somehow responsible for the trauma or that we deserved the pain. Learning to be compassionate with ourselves can be a long process, but it's an essential one.

Why Self-Compassion is Vital for Recovery

At its core, self-compassion is about recognizing that you are worthy of love, care, and kindness, no matter what you've been through. When you've experienced trauma, especially ongoing trauma, it's easy to internalize the belief that you are somehow less, that you're damaged or unworthy. But this couldn't be further from the truth.

Self-compassion is essential for recovery because it creates a space where healing can happen. When we are constantly beating ourselves up or drowning in shame and self-blame, it's almost impossible to move forward. That inner critic becomes a barrier to growth, keeping us stuck in a cycle of self-punishment and emotional pain.

By practicing self-compassion, we allow ourselves to soften. We create an environment where it's okay to not be perfect, where it's okay to make mistakes, and where it's okay to take the time we need to heal. And most importantly, we start to recognize that what happened to us is not a reflection of our worth.

I recall working with a client who had endured an abusive relationship for many years. She couldn't stop blaming herself for staying so long, for not seeing the red flags earlier. Her self-talk was filled with phrases like "I'm so stupid" and "Why didn't I leave sooner?" But when we started working on self-compassion, something shifted. She began to see herself not as someone who had failed, but as someone who had survived. She learned to talk to herself with the same empathy she would give to a friend in her situation. And with that shift, her healing journey truly began.

Self-compassion is not about excusing what happened to you or pretending everything is okay. It's about recognizing that you did the best you could with the tools and knowledge you had at the time. It's about giving yourself the grace to heal, without judgment or blame.

Overcoming Shame and Self-Blame

Shame is one of the heaviest burdens we carry after trauma. It creeps in quietly, telling us that what happened is somehow our fault, that we're defective or unlovable because of what we went through. Shame whispers that we deserved the abuse, the neglect, or the betrayal, and it convinces us that if we were just better, smarter, stronger, or more lovable, none of it would have happened.

One of the cruel tricks of trauma is that it often leaves us feeling like we are to blame. We ask ourselves over and over: "What did I do wrong?" or "Why wasn't I enough?" This self-blame becomes a familiar but toxic comfort—it gives us a false sense of control. If it was somehow our fault, maybe we could have prevented it. Perhaps we can prevent it from recurring.

But here's the hard truth: It wasn't your fault. Trauma happens to us, not because of us. Whether you experienced childhood abuse, an abusive relationship, or another form of prolonged trauma, the responsibility lies with the people who hurt you—not with you.

Yet knowing this logically doesn't always make it easier to let go of shame and self-blame. That's where self-compassion comes in. It offers a way to gently begin unraveling those tightly held beliefs, replacing self-criticism with understanding and care.

One of the most important things I've learned, both for myself and through my work, is that shame cannot survive in the light of compassion. When we start to treat ourselves with kindness, the grip of shame loosens. We stop seeing ourselves as defective or broken and start seeing ourselves as survivors, as people who went through something incredibly difficult and came out the other side.

Practical Exercises to Cultivate Self-Compassion

If you've spent years being hard on yourself, the idea of self-compassion can feel uncomfortable, or even impossible. But self-compassion, like any skill, can be cultivated with practice.

Here are some exercises to help you get started:

1. The Self-Compassion Break

This is a simple but powerful exercise to use when you're feeling overwhelmed, ashamed, or critical of yourself. It involves three steps:

- **Step 1: Acknowledge the Pain**
When you're feeling emotional pain or self-criticism, take a moment to acknowledge what's happening. Say to yourself, "This is a moment of suffering" or "I'm really struggling right now." Simply recognizing the difficulty of the moment helps create space for compassion.

- **Step 2: Remind Yourself of Common Humanity**
One of the key components of self-compassion is recognizing that you are not alone in your suffering. Everyone experiences pain, trauma, and self-doubt at some point. Say to yourself, "Suffering is a part of life" or "I'm not alone in feeling this way."

- **Step 3: Offer Yourself Kindness**
Finally, place a hand on your heart or another comforting gesture and say something kind to yourself, such as, "May I be kind to myself in this moment," or "I am worthy of love and kindness." Think about the supportive words you would give

to a close friend in a tough situation, and direct them towards yourself.

2. Write Yourself a Compassionate Letter

Writing can be a powerful way to process emotions and practice self-compassion. Try writing yourself a letter from the perspective of a compassionate friend. Imagine this friend knows everything you've been through and sees your struggles, but also knows your strength and resilience. What would they say to you? How would they remind you of your worth? Write as if you are comforting and encouraging a dear friend, then read the letter back to yourself whenever you need a reminder of your value.

3. Affirmations for Self-Compassion

Affirmations can be helpful for rewiring negative thought patterns and cultivating self-compassion. Choose a few affirmations that resonate with you and repeat them regularly, especially when self-critical thoughts arise. Here are some examples:

- "I am worthy of love and kindness."

- "I am doing the best I can, and that is enough."

- "It's okay to take care of myself."

- "I forgive myself for any mistakes I've made."

- "I deserve compassion, just like everyone else."

Write these affirmations down, keep them on your phone, or say them to yourself in front of a mirror. Over time, they can help shift your inner dialogue from one of criticism to one of compassion.

4. The Soothing Touch Exercise

Physical touch can be incredibly comforting, even when it comes from yourself. When you're feeling overwhelmed, try placing your hand over your heart, on your cheek, or hugging yourself. This simple gesture sends signals to your brain that you are safe and cared for. As you hold yourself, say something kind, like "It's okay, I'm here for you." This act of self-soothing can be a powerful way to calm your nervous system and offer yourself compassion in moments of distress.

Building self-compassion is a practice, and like all practices, it takes time. But with each small step, you're creating a foundation of kindness and care that will support you throughout your healing journey. You deserve compassion, not just from others but from yourself, and it's this self-compassion that will help you overcome shame, release self-blame, and ultimately move toward healing.

PART 2: THERAPEUTIC APPROACHES TO HEALING

Chapter 4

Relational Therapy: Healing Through Relationships

When I think about trauma, one of the first things that comes to mind is how deeply it affects our relationships. Trauma doesn't just impact how we see the world or ourselves—it changes how we connect with others. Our ability to trust, feel safe, and form healthy attachments can be deeply shaken after we've been hurt by those closest to us. Relationships, for many of us, become a source of fear rather than comfort.

Relational therapy is one of the most powerful tools in healing this part of ourselves. By focusing on the dynamics of our relationships and how we relate to others, it allows us to rebuild those broken bridges—to others and, ultimately, to ourselves.

But let's start at the beginning: How exactly does trauma affect relationships? And how does relational therapy help us navigate the complex process of learning to trust and connect again?

How Trauma Affects Relationships and Attachment Styles

Trauma, particularly Complex PTSD, can have a profound effect on how we attach to others. If you've been hurt by the very people who were supposed to protect you—parents, caregivers, partners—it's only natural that trusting others becomes a challenge. This disruption often begins early in life and influences the patterns we carry into adulthood.

There are several ways trauma affects relationships, and it often stems from how we develop attachment styles. You may have heard about attachment theory, which suggests that how we attach to our caregivers in childhood affects how we form bonds as adults. People who grow up in safe, nurturing environments often develop secure attachments. But for those of us who've experienced trauma, especially chronic or developmental trauma, our attachment styles can be deeply impacted.

- **Avoidant Attachment:** Some people, after experiencing trauma, develop an avoidant attachment style. This means they tend to distance themselves emotionally from others, often because intimacy feels threatening. They may have learned early on that relying on others leads to disappointment or hurt, so they keep their guard up, even in relationships where they desire connection.

- **Anxious Attachment:** On the other end of the spectrum is anxious attachment. Those with this style may cling to relationships, constantly worrying about abandonment or rejection. They've learned to associate love with fear—fear of being left, fear of not being enough—and this can lead to a pattern of seeking reassurance and validation from partners, sometimes to the point of self-sabotage.

- **Disorganized Attachment:** For many trauma survivors, their attachment style is disorganized—swinging between avoidance and anxiety. This is often a result of experiencing relationships that were both a source of comfort and fear. When caregivers or loved ones are unpredictable, or even abusive, the nervous system becomes confused. You may crave closeness, yet feel terrified of being hurt again, leading to a push-pull dynamic in relationships.

No matter the attachment style, the thread that runs through all of these experiences is a sense of fear and mistrust in relationships. Trauma leaves us feeling like we must either protect ourselves by keeping people at a distance or desperately seek approval and love to avoid being hurt again.

Relational Therapy and Its Role in Healing

Relational therapy is designed to heal these wounds. It focuses on how we relate to others and helps us work through the challenges that trauma creates in our relationships. Unlike some forms of therapy that concentrate solely on the individual's internal world, relational therapy places emphasis on the interactions between people. It's about understanding how trauma affects your ability to connect, and then finding ways to repair and rebuild those connections.

One of the key components of relational therapy is the therapeutic relationship itself. The relationship between you and your therapist becomes a safe space where you can begin to practice trust and vulnerability in a controlled, supportive environment. For many people who have been hurt in relationships, this is the first time they experience a relationship that is free of judgment, manipulation, or abandonment.

I remember working with a client who had experienced significant childhood trauma. She had spent her entire adult life avoiding intimate relationships, convinced that getting close to someone would only lead to more pain. In therapy, we spent months slowly building trust, not rushing the process. Through the therapeutic relationship, she began to see that not all relationships are dangerous and that it's possible to feel safe and supported by another person. Relational therapy gave her the tools to gradually re-enter the world of relationships with a new perspective—one that wasn't based on fear, but on mutual respect and trust.

Relational therapy often uses *here-and-now* techniques, where the therapist and client examine the patterns that show up within the therapeutic relationship itself. If you notice yourself pulling away or feeling anxious in session, that can be a reflection of how you respond to relationships outside of therapy. This real-time feedback allows for a deep exploration of how trauma has shaped your interactions, and it creates an opportunity to practice new ways of relating in a safe and structured space.

Learning to Rebuild Trust and Foster Healthy Relationships

Trust is a fragile thing, especially when it's been broken repeatedly. But the beautiful thing about trust is that, with time and effort, it can be rebuilt. This is one of the main goals of relational therapy—helping you learn how to trust again, both in yourself and in others.

The process of rebuilding trust isn't linear. It doesn't happen all at once, and it requires a lot of patience. But there are some key principles and practices that can help you along the way.

1. Start with Yourself

Before we can fully trust others, we need to rebuild trust in ourselves. Trauma often leaves us questioning our own judgment, instincts, and worth. We may have spent years ignoring our gut feelings or downplaying our needs to keep the peace or avoid conflict. Learning to trust yourself again means reconnecting with those inner signals—your intuition, your boundaries, your needs—and honoring them.

One exercise that can help rebuild self-trust is journaling about your emotions and decisions. Start small by writing about daily experiences—what did you feel today? What decisions did you make? How did those decisions reflect your needs and values? Over time, this practice helps you reconnect with your internal voice, making it easier to trust yourself in bigger, more complex situations.

2. Recognize and Challenge Negative Relationship Patterns

Trauma survivors often find themselves in relationships that repeat the dynamics of their past trauma. You might find yourself drawn to partners who are emotionally unavailable, critical, or controlling—echoing the behavior of an abusive parent or former partner. This isn't because you "want" to be hurt again; it's because the brain tends to seek out what's familiar, even if it's unhealthy.

Relational therapy helps you recognize these patterns and, more importantly, teaches you how to challenge and change them. By identifying what triggers your fears in relationships, you can begin to make different choices. For example, if you notice that you're drawn to people who dismiss your emotions, you can start to seek out relationships with those who are empathetic and supportive. It's a gradual process, but over time, these small changes add up to healthier and more fulfilling connections.

3. Practice Vulnerability in Safe Relationships

Vulnerability is scary, especially when it's been used against you in the past. But it's also the key to building deep, meaningful relationships. One of the most important steps in relational healing is learning to be vulnerable again, but in safe, supportive relationships.

Start small. You don't need to share your deepest fears with someone right away. Instead, practice vulnerability in small ways—ask for help when you need it, share a personal thought or feeling, or express a boundary. Over time, these small acts of vulnerability help build trust, both with yourself and with others. And in the right relationships, you'll find that your vulnerability is met with empathy and care, not judgment or rejection.

4. Cultivate Boundaries

Boundaries are essential in healthy relationships, and they are particularly important for trauma survivors. When you've been hurt or violated in the past, it can be difficult to know where your boundaries are, let alone how to enforce them. But boundaries are not just about keeping people out—they're also about protecting your own emotional well-being and creating space for connection that feels safe and respectful.

In relational therapy, you'll learn how to identify and communicate your boundaries. This might mean setting limits on how much emotional labor you take on in a relationship, or it might involve creating physical or emotional distance from people who trigger your trauma responses. Whatever the boundary, the goal is to create relationships where you feel empowered, not controlled or overwhelmed.

In the end, healing through connection is about relearning how to trust, both in yourself and in others. It's about moving away from patterns of fear and self-protection and stepping into relationships that are based on mutual respect, care, and understanding. It's not an easy process—there will be setbacks, and there will be times when it feels safer to retreat into isolation. But with the help of relational therapy and the support of safe, healthy connections, it's possible to rebuild those bridges and find a way back to trust, love, and authentic connection.

Chapter 5

Somatic Psychology: Healing Trauma Through the Body

As I mentioned earlier, one of the most profound realizations I've had about trauma is that it doesn't just live in our minds—it lives in our bodies. It took me years to understand that the anxiety, hypervigilance, and tension I was holding weren't just emotional states. They were physical sensations rooted deep in my muscles, my breath, and even my posture. Trauma leaves its mark on the body in ways that often go unnoticed, but once you start paying attention, it's undeniable. This is where somatic psychology comes in.

Somatic psychology teaches us that our bodies are not separate from our emotions. In fact, they are deeply intertwined. For trauma survivors, learning how to release trauma stored in the body is a crucial step in the healing process. It's not enough to just talk about our experiences in therapy—we need to feel them, process them, and let them go physically.

Let's go into how we can do that, using somatic techniques to connect with the body, release trauma, and promote emotional healing.

How to Release Trauma Stored in the Body

When we experience trauma, our body reacts instinctively. Whether we fight, flee, freeze, or fawn, these responses are designed to protect us. But what happens when the trauma is prolonged or unresolved? The energy that our body mobilizes in response to danger doesn't get fully released. It stays trapped inside us—often manifesting as chronic tension, pain, anxiety, or a feeling of being "stuck." This is why trauma can feel so deeply ingrained—it's not just a memory; it's something we physically carry with us.

Letting go of trauma held within the body involves allowing it to finish the cycle of stress response. In essence, it's about finishing what trauma interrupted. Think about animals in the wild—after a predator chases them, they often shake, tremble, or run to release the pent-up energy in their bodies. We, as humans, don't usually do this. Instead, we suppress those natural reactions, either because we've been taught to "hold it together" or because we don't feel safe enough to let go.

There are many ways to begin releasing trauma from the body, but the key is to do it gradually and with intention. Trauma is stored deep within the nervous system, and releasing it too quickly can feel overwhelming. The process should be gentle, allowing the body to slowly unwind its tightly-held defenses.

Introduction to Somatic Techniques

Somatic techniques are tools that help us connect with our bodies and bring awareness to where we're holding tension or trauma. These practices teach us to listen to the subtle signals our body is sending and to respond with care and compassion. Some of the most effective somatic techniques include body scanning, breathwork, and mindful movement.

1. Body Scanning

Body scanning is one of the simplest yet most powerful somatic techniques for trauma healing. It involves tuning into your body, one area at a time, and noticing what sensations are present. The goal is not to judge or change anything, but simply to observe. Attuning yourself to various areas of your body with mindfulness can help you pinpoint where tension or discomfort related to trauma may be stored.

Here's a basic body scanning exercise to try:

- **Find somewhere calm:** settle into a comfortable position, whether sitting or lying down. If it feels safe, close your eyes.

- **Start at the top of your head:** Pay attention to any sensations you experience—whether it's warmth, tension, coolness, or something different. Take a few moments to observe.

- **Move down your body:** Gradually shift your focus to different areas of your body—your forehead, face, neck, shoulders, chest, abdomen, hips, legs, and feet. Take your time with each area, noticing any tightness, pain, or numbness.

- **Direct your breath to the area of tension:** When you identify regions of discomfort, visualize your breath easing the tension with each inhalation and exhalation.

Body scanning helps you develop body awareness, which is the foundation for releasing trauma. Gaining awareness of where trauma resides in your body allows you to start releasing it through mindful focus and breathing.

2. Breathwork

Breathwork is a vital somatic technique that can help regulate the nervous system and release trauma from the body. Trauma often disrupts our natural breathing patterns—leading to shallow, rapid breaths or a sense of constriction in the chest. By consciously working with the breath, we can calm the nervous system and promote a sense of safety in the body.

One simple yet powerful breathwork practice is **diaphragmatic breathing** (also known as belly breathing). This technique encourages deep, full breaths that engage the diaphragm, helping to calm the body's fight-or-flight response.

Here's how to practice diaphragmatic breathing:

- **Find a comfortable position:** Sit or lie down in a relaxed position. Place one hand on your chest and the other on your belly.

- **Inhale deeply through your nose:** As you inhale, focus on expanding your belly rather than your chest. The hand on your belly should rise, while the hand on your chest stays relatively still.

- **Exhale slowly through your mouth:** As you exhale, let your belly fall. Try to make the exhale longer than the inhale, which helps activate the parasympathetic nervous system (the part of the nervous system responsible for relaxation).

- **Repeat for several minutes:** Continue this breathing pattern for a few minutes, paying attention to the sensation of the breath moving in and out of your body.

Breathwork helps create space for the body to release stored tension. It also signals to the nervous system that it's safe to relax, which is crucial for trauma healing.

3. Mindful Movement

Trauma can make us feel disconnected from our bodies, and one of the ways to reconnect is through mindful movement. This doesn't have to be anything intense—gentle forms of movement like yoga, stretching, or even walking can help us tune into our bodies and release trapped energy.

I've found that trauma survivors often benefit from slow, intentional movements that allow them to feel safe and grounded. **Somatic yoga** is one approach that combines movement with mindfulness, helping to release tension while cultivating body awareness.

Here's a simple mindful movement exercise you can try:

- **Stand or sit comfortably**: Start by standing or sitting in a way that feels comfortable for your body. Close your eyes if you feel comfortable doing so.

- **Begin with gentle neck rolls**: Slowly roll your head in one direction, being mindful of any areas of tension in your neck and shoulders. After a few rotations, switch directions.

- **Move your shoulders**: Gently roll your shoulders backward and forward, releasing any tightness in the upper body.

- Stretch your arms: Extend your arms overhead, reaching up as far as feels comfortable, and then gently lower them back down to your sides.

- Tune into your breath: As you move, synchronize your movements with your breath. Inhale as you lift or stretch, and exhale as you release or lower.

- Move at your own pace: This practice is about tuning into your body's needs, so move in a way that feels intuitive and nourishing for you.

The goal of mindful movement is to bring your awareness back into your body in a gentle, non-threatening way. It helps release tension and restores a sense of connection with your physical self.

Exercises to Connect Your Body and Mind

As we've discussed, trauma affects both the body and the mind, so it's essential to work with both to promote healing. Below are some practical exercises that combine body awareness with emotional healing. These techniques are intended to help with reconnecting with your body, processing your emotions, and letting go of accumulated trauma.

1. Emotional Body Scan

This exercise builds on the body scan technique but with a focus on emotional awareness. As you scan your body, pay attention to any emotions that arise in different areas.

- **Find somewhere calm:** Get into a comfortable posture, either sitting or lying down. Close your eyes if it feels secure.

- **Scan your body for sensations:** Start at your head and move slowly down to your feet, noticing any areas of tension, pain, or tightness.

- **Identify the emotions:** As you notice physical sensations, ask yourself if any emotions are attached to those areas. For example, tightness in your chest might be linked to anxiety, or tension in your jaw might be connected to anger.

- **Breathe into the emotion:** Once you've identified an emotion, take a few deep breaths and imagine releasing that emotion with each exhale. You can even visualize the emotion leaving your body as you breathe.

This exercise helps bridge the gap between body awareness and emotional processing, allowing you to release both physical and emotional tension.

2. Grounding Through Sensation

Grounding is an important tool for trauma survivors, especially when dealing with flashbacks or overwhelming emotions. This exercise uses body sensation to bring you back into the present moment and out of a trauma response.

- **Find a grounding object:** Hold an object in your hands, like a smooth stone or a soft piece of fabric.

- **Tune into the sensation:** Focus on the texture, weight, and temperature of the object. How does it feel in your hands?

- **Focus on your feet:** Bring your attention to the feeling of your feet on the ground. Notice the pressure of the floor against your feet, and feel the connection to the earth beneath you.

- **Breathe and observe:** Take a few deep breaths as you focus on these physical sensations. Allow them to anchor you in the present moment.

This practice helps regulate the nervous system by using physical sensations to bring your awareness back into the body.

3. Movement to Release Emotional Energy

When emotions feel "stuck" in your body, movement can help release them. This exercise is about using intuitive movement to express and release emotional energy.

- **Find a private space**: You'll want a space where you feel comfortable moving freely. Close your eyes if that feels safe for you.

- **Tune into your body**: Take a few deep breaths and notice any areas of tension or emotional discomfort.

- **Move intuitively**: Begin to move in a way that feels natural for your body. You might shake, stretch, sway, or dance—there's no right or wrong way to do this. Let your body guide the movement.

- **Express the emotion**: If you feel anger, you might stomp or punch the air. If you feel sadness, you might curl inward or sway gently. The goal is to let your body express the emotion in whatever way feels authentic.

- **Rest and reflect**: After a few minutes of movement, come to a still position and take a few deep breaths. Reflect on how your body feels now compared to when you started.

This exercise will help in releasing accumulated emotional energy and reestablishing a connection with your body's natural rhythms.

Healing trauma is not just a mental or emotional process—it's a physical one. By using somatic techniques like body scanning, breathwork, and mindful movement, we can begin to release the trauma stored in our bodies and reclaim our sense of safety and connection. Remember, this is a gradual process. There's no need to rush. Be gentle with yourself as you explore these practices, and trust that your body knows how to heal.

Chapter 6

Cognitive Behavioral Therapy (CBT) for Trauma Recovery

When I first began to unpack the ways trauma had shaped my life, one thing became crystal clear—my thoughts were not my friends. I don't know about you, but when I think about how trauma impacts us, the physical scars aren't always the most damaging. It's the way trauma distorts how we think about ourselves, others, and the world around us. The negative thought patterns that trauma creates can feel like an invisible prison, keeping us stuck in cycles of fear, shame, and hopelessness. This is where Cognitive Behavioral Therapy (CBT) comes into play, and let me tell you, it's a game-changer.

CBT is a well-established therapeutic approach that works by identifying and challenging those unhelpful thoughts and beliefs that keep us tied to our trauma. It's like giving your brain a reset button, teaching it to think in a healthier, more realistic way. The beauty of CBT is that it's incredibly practical—you don't need to rely on abstract theories to see real, tangible changes in your life. Instead, you learn to actively reshape your thoughts, which in turn reshapes your emotional and behavioral responses to trauma.

Let's go into how trauma shapes our thinking, how CBT helps us challenge these thought patterns, and some specific exercises you can try to begin reframing your trauma-related thoughts.

How Trauma Shapes Negative Thought Patterns

Trauma has a sneaky way of embedding itself in our minds, shaping how we see ourselves and the world. After experiencing trauma, it's common for survivors to develop what's called negative automatic thoughts—those recurring, often unconscious thoughts that pop up without us even realizing. These thoughts are typically skewed toward the negative, leaving us stuck in patterns of self-blame, hypervigilance, and fear.

In my own experience, after going through a particularly rough period, I found myself constantly thinking things like, "I'm not good enough," or "I'll never be safe." These weren't just passing thoughts—they were ingrained beliefs that shaped how I moved through the world. They made me avoid certain situations, feel anxious around people, and struggle with confidence.

The tricky part is that trauma can make these negative thoughts feel **true**—so true that we don't question them. But the reality is, they're often based on fear, not fact. Trauma distorts our perception, making us think the world is more dangerous, or that we're more powerless than we really are.

Using CBT to Challenge Unhelpful Thoughts and Beliefs

This is where CBT comes in. The central idea behind CBT is that our thoughts, feelings, and behaviors are all interconnected. If we can change how we think about a situation, we can change how we feel and ultimately how we respond to it. For trauma survivors, CBT offers tools to **challenge the unhelpful thoughts** that trauma has planted in our minds.

Here's an example from my own life. After a traumatic experience, I often felt overwhelmed by a sense of helplessness, thinking things like, "Nothing I do will ever change what happened." This belief would spiral into feelings of depression and avoidance. But through CBT, I learned to identify this thought as distorted—just because something bad happened in the past doesn't mean I have no control over my present or future. By challenging the thought and reframing it, I began to take small steps toward regaining a sense of agency.

CBT focuses on identifying **cognitive distortions**—the ways our mind tricks us into thinking negatively—and teaching us how to counter them. Some common cognitive distortions trauma survivors experience include:

- **Catastrophizing:** Always expecting the worst possible outcome ("I'll never recover from this").

- **Black-and-white thinking:** Seeing situations in extremes, with no middle ground ("If I'm not perfect, I'm a failure").

- **Overgeneralization:** Drawing broad conclusions based on one negative event ("I failed once, so I'll always fail").

- **Emotional reasoning:** This involves treating feelings as if they are facts, such as thinking, "I am afraid, so there must be danger."

Once you start recognizing these distortions, you can begin to challenge them. CBT teaches you to ask questions like:

- Is this thought based on fact or fear?

- What evidence supports or contradicts this belief?

- Is there another way to look at this situation?

- What would I tell a friend who was thinking this way?

By questioning the validity of our thoughts, we can start to see them for what they are—just thoughts, not absolute truths. This process of challenging and reframing negative thoughts is empowering. It gives us back control over our minds, something trauma often takes away.

CBT Exercises for Reframing Trauma-Related Thinking

Now, let's get into some practical exercises. These are techniques you can try on your own to start challenging and reframing your trauma-related thoughts.

1. Thought Record Exercise

One of the most effective CBT tools for identifying and challenging negative thoughts is the thought record. This exercise helps you break down your thoughts and analyze them logically, so you can see where they might be distorted.

Here's how to do it:

- **Identify the situation:** Write down the specific situation that triggered your negative thoughts. Be as detailed as possible.

- **Record your automatic thoughts:** List the thoughts that came up in response to the situation, such as believing statements like, "I am a failure," or "Things will never improve."

- **Write down the emotions:** What emotions did these thoughts trigger? Were you anxious, sad, angry?

- **Challenge the thought:** Now, question the thought. Is it based on facts, or is it a cognitive distortion? Seek out evidence that either backs up or refutes this belief. Ask the question, "Is there a more balanced perspective on this issue?"

- **Reframe the thought**: Replace the original thought with a more realistic, balanced one. For example, instead of "I'll never get better," you might reframe it as "Recovery takes time, but I'm making progress."

This exercise helps you gain distance from your thoughts, giving you the perspective needed to challenge and change them.

2. Cognitive Restructuring

Cognitive restructuring is a core CBT technique that helps you break down unhelpful beliefs and replace them with healthier ones. This exercise is especially helpful when you're dealing with deeply ingrained trauma-related beliefs like, "I'm worthless," or "I can't trust anyone."

Here's how to practice cognitive restructuring:

- **Identify the core belief**: Start by identifying a core negative belief you have about yourself or the world as a result of trauma. For example, "I'm unlovable."

- **Find evidence for and against the belief**: Make two columns on a piece of paper. In one column, list all the evidence that supports the belief. In the other, list evidence that contradicts it. You'll often find that there's much more evidence against the belief than for it.

- **Create a balanced belief:** Based on the evidence, create a more balanced belief. For example, instead of "I'm unlovable," you might reframe it as, "I've been hurt in the past, but that doesn't mean I'm unlovable. I deserve love and care."

This process helps you dismantle deeply rooted negative beliefs and replace them with healthier, more empowering ones.

3. Behavioral Activation

Sometimes, trauma leaves us stuck in a cycle of avoidance. We avoid situations, people, or places that remind us of the trauma, and this avoidance only reinforces our negative thoughts. Behavioral activation is a CBT technique that helps break this cycle by encouraging us to take small, positive actions—even when we don't feel like it.

Here's how to practice behavioral activation:

- **Identify an activity you've been avoiding:** It could be something as simple as going for a walk, calling a friend, or working on a project. Choose something that feels manageable but still challenges your avoidance.

- **Set a small, achievable goal**: Start small. If you've been avoiding social situations, your goal could be to send a text to a friend rather than meeting them in person.

- **Track your mood**: Before and after completing the activity, check in with yourself. How did you feel before? How did you feel after? Often, taking action helps shift our mood in a positive direction, even if it's just a small improvement.

Behavioral activation helps us challenge the avoidance patterns that keep us trapped in negative thoughts, and it reinforces the idea that we have the power to take action and create positive change.

4. Imagery Rescripting

For trauma survivors who experience intrusive memories or flashbacks, imagery rescripting is a CBT technique that can help change how these memories are stored and experienced. This exercise involves revisiting a traumatic memory but altering the ending in a way that feels more empowering or comforting.

Here's how to try imagery rescripting:

- **Choose a memory**: Start by choosing a memory that feels safe enough to revisit. It's important not to choose something too overwhelming, especially if you're doing this on your own.

- **Reimagine the memory**: Close your eyes and picture the memory as clearly as possible. Now, imagine changing the ending. You might imagine yourself being rescued, or you might picture yourself standing up to someone who hurt you.

- **Focus on the new outcome**: Spend a few minutes focusing on the new, more positive outcome. Notice how it feels in your body to change the ending.

This technique can help reduce the emotional intensity of traumatic memories by allowing you to take control of how they're experienced.

CBT is an incredibly powerful tool for trauma recovery because it puts the power back in your hand to view life the way you want to, rather than the way your trauma makes you.

Chapter 7

Eye Movement Desensitization and Reprocessing (EMDR)

EMDR is a structured therapy with deep roots in understanding how trauma gets stuck in our brains and bodies. And what makes it particularly interesting is that it doesn't require you to relive your trauma over and over again. Instead, it allows you to process those painful memories in a way that lessens their grip on your emotional well-being.

In this chapter, we'll explore what EMDR is, how it works, when it might be the right option in your recovery journey, and how to prepare for EMDR sessions so you can get the most out of this powerful healing tool.

EMDR and How It Works to Heal Trauma

Eye Movement Desensitization and Reprocessing (EMDR) is a therapeutic method created in the late 1980s by Francine Shapiro. It's primarily used to help individuals process and heal from trauma, but its applications have expanded to include anxiety, depression, phobias, and even performance anxiety. The core idea behind EMDR is that traumatic experiences can become "stuck" in our brain's memory processing system, leading to ongoing distress even years after the event has passed. EMDR helps to "unstick" these memories, allowing them to be processed in a healthier way.

The fascinating part of EMDR is how it taps into the brain's natural healing processes. When we experience something traumatic, our brain doesn't always get a chance to process the event properly. It's as though the memory is stored in a raw, unprocessed form, along with all the emotions, physical sensations, and negative beliefs that came with it. This is why, even long after the event, trauma can feel as fresh as if it happened yesterday.

During EMDR, the therapist guides you through recalling the traumatic event while engaging in a form of bilateral stimulation—usually, this involves following their finger or a light with your eyes, moving them back and forth. This bilateral stimulation activates both sides of the brain, which helps to process the trauma in a more adaptive way. As a result, the emotional intensity of the memory decreases, and the negative beliefs attached to it can be reframed into something more positive.

Here's a simple analogy: Imagine you're trying to close a tab on your computer, but it's frozen. The memory of your trauma is like that frozen tab, preventing you from moving forward. EMDR is like a reset button that allows your brain to unfreeze, close the tab, and move on.

When EMDR is Appropriate in Your Recovery Journey

EMDR can be an incredibly effective tool, but it's not always the first step in trauma recovery. It's often best used when you've already done some foundational work on stabilizing your emotions and building coping mechanisms. That said, it's suitable for a wide range of trauma-related conditions, and many people find relief with it even when other therapies haven't worked as well.

So, when is EMDR the right choice?

1. When Trauma Feels "Stuck"

A strong indicator that EMDR could be suitable is when you sense that your trauma is persistently "stuck" in your mind. You might have tried other forms of therapy, but the memories, flashbacks, or physical responses still feel overwhelming and unresolved. If you find that even after talking about your trauma, it still triggers the same intense emotions and reactions, EMDR could help by facilitating deeper processing.

2. When You're Ready to Confront Trauma, But Without Reliving It

Unlike some forms of therapy, EMDR doesn't require you to go into explicit detail about your trauma. You won't have to describe every moment of what happened if that feels too overwhelming. Instead, you'll focus on the emotions, sensations, and beliefs connected to the memory, which can make it a gentler option for those who aren't ready to fully relive their trauma.

3. When You've Developed Some Coping Skills

EMDR can be intense, and it's important to have some emotional tools in your toolbox before starting. This might mean having a solid grounding practice, mindfulness techniques, or a strong support network. If you're at a point in your recovery where you've learned to manage your emotional responses, EMDR could be the next step to resolving deeper, more entrenched trauma.

4. When Traditional Talk Therapy Feels Incomplete

Some people find that talk therapy alone doesn't fully address the impact of trauma. You may understand intellectually what happened to you, but the emotional and somatic (body-based) responses still linger. EMDR engages both the emotional and somatic aspects of trauma, making it a great option for those who feel like they've hit a wall in talk therapy.

Guided Exercises to Prepare for EMDR Sessions

Before diving into EMDR, it's helpful to have some preparatory exercises under your belt. These exercises are designed to help you get the most out of your sessions by building self-awareness, emotional resilience, and grounding skills.

1. Safe Place Visualization

One of the key components of EMDR preparation is creating a "safe place" in your mind—a mental sanctuary you can go to when things feel overwhelming during or after a session. This safe place acts as a calming anchor, providing a sense of security when emotions rise to the surface.

Here's how to create your safe place:

- **Choose a calm place** where you will not be interrupted. Close your eyes and imagine a place where you feel completely safe, calm, and at peace. It can be real or imagined—a beach, a forest, or even a cozy room.

- **Engage all your senses.** What do you see, hear, smell, feel, and taste in this safe place? The more vivid your visualization, the more effective it will be when you need it.

- **Practice returning to this place** regularly, especially when you feel stressed or anxious. Over time, it will become a reliable resource during your EMDR sessions.

2. Mindful Breathing

Because EMDR can sometimes bring up intense emotions, having a grounding practice like mindful breathing can be incredibly helpful. Mindful breathing helps you stay present in your body and regulate your nervous system during sessions.

Here's a simple mindful breathing exercise:

- Sit or lie down in a comfortable position. Close your eyes if that feels okay for you.

- Bring your attention to your breath. Pay attention to the feeling of air flowing in and out of your nostrils or mouth.

- Begin by inhaling deeply through your nose at a slow pace, counting to four. Hold the breath for a moment, and then exhale slowly through your mouth, counting to four again.

- As you breathe, focus on the rise and fall of your chest or the feeling of the breath moving through your body. If your thoughts drift, gently redirect your focus back to your breathing. Practice this for five minutes each day, and use it during EMDR sessions if things get overwhelming.

3. Body Awareness

Since EMDR involves working with both the mind and body, it's helpful to start developing awareness of your body's sensations before you begin. This will make it easier to notice when certain memories or emotions trigger physical reactions during sessions.

Try this body awareness exercise:

- **Sit comfortably** and close your eyes. Begin by taking several deep breaths to help you center yourself.

- **Conduct a body scan** from head to toe, noting any areas of tension, discomfort, or relaxation. Notice where you feel tight, where you feel loose, and where you might be holding your emotions.

- **Breathe into the areas of tension,** imagining that your breath is gently softening and releasing the tightness.

Practice this body scan daily to increase your awareness of how your body responds to stress and emotions. This awareness will help you stay grounded during your EMDR sessions.

EMDR is a truly transformative therapy for trauma recovery. It provides a structured way to work through those memories and feelings that have remained unresolved, often for years. What I love most about EMDR is that it doesn't just leave you with insight—it leaves you with healing.

And while it can be a powerful tool, it's important to go into it with a sense of readiness, patience, and self-compassion. Trauma recovery is a journey, and EMDR is one of the many steps that can bring you closer to a more peaceful, grounded life.

Chapter 8

Distress Tolerance: Emotional Regulation and Resilience

Let me start by saying this: resilience isn't about never feeling overwhelmed. It's not about being tough or "strong" in the way we sometimes think of those words. Real resilience is about learning how to survive the storm, even when it feels like it's never going to end. It's the ability to tolerate distress, to sit with discomfort, and to keep going, even when life feels unbearable. In the context of trauma, distress tolerance can feel like an impossible skill to master, but I'm here to tell you it's not only possible—it's one of the most powerful tools in your recovery toolkit.

Trauma has a way of leaving us on edge, easily overwhelmed by stress or emotion. The ability to withstand distress without reacting impulsively or shutting down is the foundation of building long-term resilience. While the journey to distress tolerance can be bumpy, it starts with small steps, which, over time, add up to significant emotional strength.

In this chapter, we'll break down techniques that can help you build emotional and mental resilience, dive into Dialectical Behavior Therapy (DBT) skills designed specifically for distress tolerance, and work through step-by-step exercises to manage and tolerate difficult emotions.

Increasing Your Emotional and Mental Resilience

When I work with people recovering from trauma, I often hear them say they wish they could avoid the emotional rollercoaster. They want to feel calm and steady, but the reality of trauma recovery is that emotions can be unpredictable and overwhelming. The first step in building resilience is understanding that emotional storms are part of the process—and resilience doesn't mean you avoid them, it means you learn to navigate through them.

1. Radical Acceptance

One of the most important tools in building resilience is radical acceptance. This is the idea that we don't have to like or approve of what's happening, but we do need to accept that it *is* happening. Trauma survivors often battle with "why" questions—Why did this happen to me? Why can't I feel normal? Why am I still hurting? While these questions are valid, getting stuck in them often increases distress. Radical acceptance teaches us to accept our current reality without judgment.

Here's how you can start practicing radical acceptance:

- **Acknowledge the present moment.** Instead of fighting against what's happening, notice it. Say to yourself, "This is hard, but it's happening."

- **Let go of the "shoulds."** Often, distress comes from thinking that things should be different. Practice letting go of the need for things to be a certain way. Rather than saying, "This shouldn't be occurring," consider saying, "This is what is happening."

- **Practice mindfulness.** Radical acceptance pairs well with mindfulness, which is simply observing your thoughts and emotions without judgment.

2. Distraction Techniques

Sometimes, when emotions are too intense, we need temporary relief—just a little space to breathe. Healthy distractions can give your brain a break, reducing the risk of reacting impulsively or becoming overwhelmed. Distraction doesn't mean avoidance, but sometimes it's a crucial tool in helping you cope in the moment.

Simple distractions you can try:

- **Do something with your hands.** Whether it's knitting, drawing, or washing dishes, engaging your hands can help shift your focus away from the distressing emotion.

- **Focus on something external.** Try the "5-4-3-2-1" grounding technique.

- **Engage in an activity you enjoy.** Watch a favorite TV show, call a friend, or go for a walk.

It's not about ignoring the emotion forever but creating enough space to tolerate it better.

3. Self-Soothing Techniques

Sometimes, building resilience isn't about solving the problem right away; it's about learning to soothe yourself in the face of distress. When emotions are running high, it helps to engage your senses in comforting ways.

Here's a simple self-soothing practice:

- **Create a calm environment.** Light a candle, wrap yourself in a cozy blanket, and dim the lights. This physical comfort can provide emotional comfort.

- **Engage your senses.** Hold something soft, listen to calming music, or make a cup of tea. Bringing your attention to soothing sensory experiences can shift your focus from the distressing emotion.

- Practice gentle self-talk. Talk to yourself with the same kindness you would offer a close friend. Phrases such as, "It's okay to feel this way. You are doing your best," can help shift your emotional perspective.

DBT Skills for Distress Tolerance

Dialectical Behavior Therapy (DBT) is a form of cognitive-behavioral therapy specifically designed to help people manage intense emotions. One of DBT's core focuses is distress tolerance, which is the ability to survive a crisis without making the situation worse.

Distress tolerance is all about learning how to accept, find meaning in, and tolerate distress. DBT doesn't aim to eliminate negative emotions but rather to help you navigate them without being overwhelmed. This skill set is invaluable when recovering from trauma because it teaches you how to ride the waves of intense emotions without letting them drown you.

TIPP (Temperature, Intense Exercise, Paced Breathing, Progressive Relaxation):

- Temperature: Pour cold water on your face or put an ice cube on your palm and squeeze it. The cold triggers a biological response that can slow down overwhelming emotions.

- Intense Exercise: A burst of physical activity like jumping jacks or running can help release pent-up energy and emotion.

- Paced Breathing: Inhale slowly for four counts, hold for four counts, and exhale for four counts. This regulates your body's stress response.

- Progressive Relaxation: Contract each muscle group for a few seconds, then relax. This helps relieve physical tension associated with emotional distress.

- Self-Soothe with the Senses: Focus on each of your five senses to bring yourself back to the present. Use soothing smells, comforting touch, and calming sights to reduce emotional overwhelm.

IMPROVE the Moment:

- Imagery: Imagine a safe place or visualize yourself overcoming the distress.

- Meaning: Find some meaning in the situation, no matter how small.

- Prayer: This can be religious or secular. Focus on something greater than yourself.

- Relaxation: Practice deep breathing or meditation.

- One Thing in the Moment: Focus on one thing you can control right now.

- Vacation: Take a short break, even if it's just mentally stepping away for five minutes.

- Encouragement: Talk to yourself as you would a friend. Offer yourself compassionate encouragement.

Step-by-Step Exercises for Tolerating Difficult Emotions

Distress tolerance exercises are designed to help you survive emotional crises without resorting to harmful behaviors or making the situation worse. Here are two powerful exercises to help you stay grounded and manage your emotions when trauma feels overwhelming.

1. The STOP Skill

The STOP skill is a simple yet powerful tool from DBT that helps you avoid reacting impulsively to intense emotions.

- S—Stop: When you feel the wave of emotion coming, stop whatever you're doing. Don't react right away.

- T—Take a Step Back: Take a breath, and step back from the situation. This creates a pause between the emotion and your reaction.

- O—Observe: Notice what's happening inside of you and around you. What thoughts are running through your mind? How does your body feel? Are there physical sensations that come with the emotion?

- P—Proceed Mindfully: Once you've observed your thoughts and emotions, choose how to proceed. Deliberately choose how you wish to react in the situation.

2. Urge Surfing

Urge surfing is a distress tolerance skill that helps you manage intense cravings or urges—whether it's the urge to self-harm, avoid, or lash out. Imagine the emotion or urge as a wave you're riding. Rather than resisting or reacting, you let the emotion pass naturally, like a wave.

- **Acknowledge the urge.** Label the feeling by saying, "I have the urge to..."

- **Notice where the urge is in your body.** Is your chest tight? Are your hands shaking? Observe how your body physically responds to the emotion.

- **Visualize the urge as a wave.** Imagine yourself riding the wave of the emotion. It may rise, but eventually, it will fall.

- **Ride it out.** Allow yourself to experience the emotion without giving in to it. Trust that, like a wave, it will pass.

Developing Emotional Regulation

When trauma strikes, one of the first things to go is our ability to regulate our emotions. Instead of responding to stressors in a balanced way, we might find ourselves overreacting, shutting down, or swinging between emotional extremes. Trauma disrupts the brain's natural ability to regulate emotions, often leaving us feeling out of control.

Learning emotional regulation is essential to healing, and it begins with small, consistent practices.

1. Breathing Techniques for Emotional Regulation

Breath is one of the most accessible and powerful tools for regulating emotions. When we're anxious, scared, or overwhelmed, our breath becomes shallow and rapid, which triggers a stress response in the body. Deep, controlled breathing sends signals to the brain that we're safe, helping to calm the nervous system.

Try this simple breathing exercise:

- Settle into a relaxed posture and gently close your eyes.

- Slowly breathe in through your nose, counting to four.

- Pause and hold your breath for four counts.

- Gently exhale through your mouth, again counting to four.

- Pay attention to the parts of your body where you feel the sensation of the urge.

2. Guided Imagery for Calmness

Guided imagery is another powerful tool for emotional regulation. It involves using mental images to evoke a sense of calm and safety. This can be especially helpful during moments of intense emotional distress when it feels like the world is spinning out of control.

Here's a guided imagery exercise you can try:

- Close your eyes and imagine a peaceful place. This could be a real location you've been to or a place you create in your mind.

- Picture yourself in this place. What do you see? Hear? Smell? Imagine the warmth of the sun on your skin or the sound of the ocean waves.

- Stay in this place for a few minutes, focusing on the calming sensations it brings.

3. Cognitive Reframing

Another essential aspect of emotional regulation is cognitive reframing, which involves shifting your perspective on a situation to reduce emotional distress. Instead of catastrophizing or jumping to the worst-case scenario, practice finding alternative ways to view the situation.

For example, if you're feeling overwhelmed by a task, instead of thinking, "I can't handle this," try reframing it to, "This is hard, but I can take it one step at a time."

Building distress tolerance and emotional regulation takes time and practice, but with each small step, you'll start to notice a difference. The key is to approach these skills with patience and self-compassion—recovery is a process, not a race. You'll have days when it feels like you're making progress and others when it feels like you're back at square one. That's okay. The important thing is that you keep moving forward, no matter how small the steps.

PART 3: BREAKING FREE FROM TRAUMA BONDS AND CYCLES

Chapter 9

Healing and Breaking Free from Abuse and Neglect

Breaking free from abuse and neglect is one of the hardest things anyone can do. I know from both personal experience and working with others that it's not just about leaving the situation physically, but emotionally and mentally disentangling yourself from the web of trauma that binds you to it. Abuse and neglect, whether from childhood or in adult relationships, can erode your sense of self, making it difficult to even recognize the need to break free. But healing is possible—it takes time, patience, and often guidance, but every small step toward reclaiming your identity is a victory.

Let's go into how you can identify trauma bonds and abusive patterns, practical steps for rebuilding your sense of identity, and how to develop healthy boundaries that will protect you as you move forward.

How to Identify and Break Free from Trauma Bonds and Abusive Relationships

A major challenge in recovering from abuse is initially recognizing that you are involved in a toxic or abusive relationship. Trauma bonds can be so deeply ingrained that you mistake them for love, loyalty, or a connection you can't live without. These bonds form when intermittent reinforcement (periods of kindness mixed with cruelty) keeps you hooked, making you feel as though leaving will deprive you of something essential. But these relationships are toxic and breaking free starts with awareness.

Signs of a Trauma Bond

1. **Constant justification of mistreatment.** If you find yourself frequently excusing or rationalizing someone's abusive behavior—whether it's emotional, verbal, or physical—you may be in a trauma bond.

2. **Feeling responsible for their actions.** Do you believe their behavior is your fault? That if you were better, more loving, or more compliant, they wouldn't treat you this way? Abusers often manipulate their victims into feeling like the problem lies with them.

3. **Inability to leave, despite harm.** Even though you know the relationship is harmful, leaving feels impossible. You might feel physically or financially trapped, but more often than not, the emotional grip is the strongest.

4. **Fleeting moments of "love" or affection.** In trauma bonds, moments of kindness or affection, however rare, can be enough to keep you stuck. These moments reinforce the hope that things will change or that the abuser isn't "all bad."

5. **Fear of being alone.** Many trauma survivors stay in abusive relationships because of a deep fear of abandonment, loneliness, or being unlovable.

Once you've identified that you're in a trauma bond, the next step is breaking free, which is often the most difficult part.

Practical Steps for Breaking Free

1. **Educate Yourself on Abuse Dynamics:** The more you learn about trauma bonds, narcissistic abuse, or neglect, the clearer the patterns will become. Education can be incredibly empowering. I personally found that once I understood the tactics of manipulation and control, I could see the dynamics more objectively, which allowed me to start taking steps away from the toxic cycle.

2. **Create Physical and Emotional Distance:** Breaking free from a trauma bond often requires creating distance. This may mean going "no contact" if it's safe, or at the very least, establishing firm boundaries (which we'll talk about shortly).

Limit communication and exposure to the abuser, even if your mind keeps pulling you back.

3. **Seek Support:** Trauma bonds are hard to break alone. You need a support system—whether it's friends, family, or a therapist—who can help you stay grounded. Share your experience with those you trust, and let them help you through the difficult moments when you're tempted to return to the toxic relationship.

4. **Focus on Self-Care and Stability:** When you're stuck in a cycle of abuse, it's easy to lose sight of basic self-care. Start by focusing on your immediate needs—sleep, nutrition, exercise, and emotional well-being. Rebuilding yourself starts with these small acts of nurturing your body and mind.

5. **Set a Plan for Exit:** If you're still in the relationship, plan your exit carefully. This might involve saving money, finding alternative living arrangements, or even seeking legal help. Having a clear plan makes the process less overwhelming, and you can focus on one step at a time rather than feeling like you need to make a sudden break all at once.

Practical Steps for Rebuilding Your Sense of Identity and Autonomy

After breaking free from abuse, one of the biggest challenges is figuring out who you are outside of the relationship. Trauma can leave your sense of identity fractured. You may have spent so much time focused on surviving or pleasing the other person that you've lost sight of your own wants, needs, and passions. Rebuilding your sense of self is a crucial step toward healing.

1. Start with Small Acts of Autonomy

When you've been in an abusive relationship, it's easy to forget that you can make decisions for yourself. Start small: pick out your own clothes, decide what you want to eat for dinner, or choose how you want to spend your free time. These small decisions remind you that you have control over your life.

2. Explore Your Interests Again

Abusers often isolate their victims, cutting them off from hobbies, passions, and even social connections. This is the time to rediscover and reconnect with the aspects of yourself that have been neglected. Ask yourself: what do I enjoy doing? What have I always wanted to try? Maybe it's something as simple as picking up a hobby you used to love or trying out a new activity you've always been curious about.

I remember a time after leaving an unhealthy relationship when I couldn't even figure out what I liked. So, I just started trying things—cooking classes, hiking, painting. Each new experience helped me rediscover a little more of who I am.

3. Journal for Self-Discovery

Writing is a valuable tool for introspection and recovery. Use a journal to articulate your feelings, thoughts, and experiences. Write about who you were before the abuse and who you want to become. Ask yourself:

- What do I value?

- What makes me feel fulfilled?

  What types of relationships do I see myself having now?

4. Reconnect with Supportive People

Abuse often isolates us from friends and loved ones. Reaching out to people who care about you, who respect your boundaries, and who genuinely support your well-being can help you rebuild a healthy sense of connection.

Being around supportive, positive relationships strengthens your evolving sense of self.

5. Set Goals for the Future

Once you start to reconnect with yourself, set small goals to move forward. These could be related to your career, education, personal development, or relationships. Setting goals helps you focus on the future and gives you something to strive for outside of your past trauma. Your goals could be as straightforward as "I aim to speak more confidently" or "I want to travel alone to become more independent."

How to Develop Healthy Boundaries

Learning to set boundaries is one of the most crucial skills to cultivate after exiting an abusive relationship. Boundaries are about protecting yourself—emotionally, physically, and mentally. When you've been in a relationship where boundaries were disrespected or trampled over, learning to set and maintain them can feel strange or uncomfortable. But healthy boundaries are key to ensuring that future relationships are respectful and balanced.

1. Understand Your Rights

A big part of setting boundaries is understanding what you're entitled to in any relationship. You are entitled to refuse, to be respected, to have your needs and emotions acknowledged, and to safeguard your emotional and physical well-being. You do not owe anyone unlimited access to your time, energy, or emotions.

2. Start by Defining Your Boundaries

Reflect on what you require in relationships to feel secure and valued. Boundaries can be about:

- **Time:** How much time you're willing to dedicate to someone.

- **Emotional:** How much emotional energy you're willing to invest in someone, especially in terms of listening or supporting them.

- **Physical:** What level of physical closeness or affection you're comfortable with.

- **Communication:** How you want to be spoken to and what's off-limits in conversations.

Write down your boundaries, and don't be afraid to revise them as you grow.

3. Practice Assertiveness

Communicating your boundaries takes practice, especially if you've been conditioned to put others' needs ahead of your own. When setting a boundary, use "I" statements and keep it simple. For example, "I need some alone time this weekend to recharge," or "I'm not comfortable discussing this right now." Assertiveness doesn't mean being aggressive—it's about being clear, calm, and firm in expressing what you need.

4. Recognize and Enforce Consequences

A boundary isn't truly a boundary unless it has a consequence. If someone crosses a line, it's important to enforce the boundary. This could mean temporarily stepping back from the relationship, having a direct conversation about what's unacceptable, or, in some cases, ending the relationship entirely if the boundary violations are consistent and harmful.

It's hard to enforce boundaries, especially when you care about the other person, but it's essential to your well-being. Over time, this will become second nature, and you'll feel more confident in standing up for yourself.

5. Surround Yourself with People Who Respect Your Boundaries

As you heal and develop a stronger sense of self, you'll naturally start to gravitate toward people who respect your boundaries. Pay attention to how others respond when you set a boundary—if they respect it, they're likely to be supportive, healthy relationships. If they push back, make excuses, or dismiss your needs, that's a red flag.

Healing from abuse and neglect is a journey, one that involves recognizing the toxic dynamics in your life, breaking free, and reclaiming your sense of self. It's not an easy path, but with each step, you rebuild your autonomy, your resilience, and your hope for a better future. Boundaries will be your shield as you move forward, allowing you to protect your growing sense of identity and ensuring that future relationships are built on respect and care.

Chapter 10

Reclaiming Your Sense of Safety and Control

One of the hardest things to regain after experiencing trauma is a sense of safety. Whether it's emotional, psychological, or physical trauma, it leaves us feeling exposed and powerless. I know this well—it took me years to realize that trauma isn't just about what happened in the past; it's about how it continues to affect you, especially your sense of safety in your own body and environment. The good news is that you *can* reclaim that safety and control, even if it feels impossible at times.

This process isn't linear—it's more like slowly building a shelter for yourself, piece by piece. So today, let's talk about how to relearn safety in your body, re-establish control in your daily life, and build a supportive environment that nurtures your healing.

Learning to Feel Safe in Your Own Body Again

When trauma happens, your body can become a battlefield. The stress response—whether it's fight, flight, freeze, or fawn—often gets stuck on "high alert." Even when the threat is no longer present, your nervous system continues to act as if it is. This makes it hard to feel at home in your body. Instead of being a place of peace, your body may feel like it's constantly on edge, bracing for the next danger.

I've found that learning to feel safe in your body again is a slow, gentle process. It's about giving yourself permission to start small and honoring your body's pace. You don't need to push yourself too hard—safety is found in ease, not in force.

1. Body Awareness and Grounding

One of the first steps to feeling safe again is reconnecting with your body through gentle awareness practices. This can be as simple as checking in with your body throughout the day.

Start with a body scan, which helps you notice where tension or discomfort may be stored. Begin at your feet and slowly move your attention upward—ask yourself, "How does this part of my body feel right now." There's no need to change anything—simply take note of what you observe. If you feel a tightness in your chest, heaviness in your legs, or a knot in your stomach, recognize it without judgment. This is your body's way of communicating.

Grounding exercises are also helpful in creating a sense of safety. Try placing your feet flat on the floor, feeling the solid ground beneath you, and take slow, deep breaths.

Tell yourself, "In this moment, I am safe." This might sound simple, but consciously grounding yourself helps calm your nervous system and reminds your body that it's not in danger right now.

2. Gentle Movement

Moving your body in a gentle, intentional way can help release tension and remind you that you're in control. Activities like yoga, tai chi, or even a slow walk can be incredibly healing. When I first started incorporating movement into my healing process, I noticed how disconnected I felt from my body at first—it was almost like I didn't trust it. But over time, I began to feel more in tune with my body's rhythms and signals.

You don't need to follow any strict routines here—the key is to move in ways that feel good and restorative. If a walk outside feels like too much, you can start by stretching at home or doing some light breathing exercises. The goal is to slowly build trust in your body again.

3. Breathing for Calm and Safety

Trauma often impacts our breath. When we're stressed or afraid, we tend to breathe shallowly, which can reinforce feelings of anxiety. Learning to breathe deeply and consciously is one of the most powerful tools you have for calming your nervous system.

Try this: Take a slow, deep breath in through your nose, hold for a few seconds, and then exhale slowly through your mouth. Repeat this a few times, and notice how it affects your body. Breathing exercises are portable—you can do them anywhere, anytime. Over time, this practice helps signal to your body that it's okay to relax and that you are in control of your breath and, by extension, your safety.

Re-establishing Control Over Your Life Through Daily Routines

Trauma can make life feel chaotic, disorganized, and overwhelming. Part of healing involves re-establishing a sense of control over your life. One of the simplest, yet most effective ways to do this is by creating daily routines.

I know from personal experience that routines can be a lifesaver. They provide structure and predictability, which helps calm the mind and gives you something concrete to hold onto when everything else feels uncertain.

1. Start Small and Build Consistency

If you're coming out of a period of trauma or chaos, it's important to start small. Don't try to overhaul your entire life all at once—it's not necessary, and it's likely to lead to frustration. Instead, begin with one or two manageable habits. Maybe it's waking up at the same time each day, or dedicating 10 minutes each morning to quiet reflection or journaling.

These small acts create a sense of consistency and predictability, which is exactly what your nervous system craves after trauma. Over time, you can build on this foundation by adding more elements to your routine. But remember, the goal is not perfection—it's about creating a rhythm that feels safe and supportive for *you*.

2. Set Simple, Achievable Goals

Incorporating small, daily goals into your routine helps you reclaim control. When trauma steals your sense of agency, even the smallest wins can feel like huge victories. I often recommend setting goals that are realistic and achievable. For example, if you're struggling to get out of bed in the morning, set a goal to simply sit up, take a few deep breaths, and acknowledge that you've made progress.

Document your goals and monitor your advancement regularly. This creates a sense of accomplishment, which reinforces the feeling that you're taking control of your life again.

3. Mindful Routines

Infusing mindfulness into your daily tasks can deepen your sense of control. Whether it's preparing a meal, taking a shower, or even brushing your teeth, slowing down and paying attention to these simple acts brings you into the present moment. You're not stuck in the past or lost in worries about the future—you're right here, doing something that supports your well-being.

Exercises for Building a Support System for Your Healing Process

Healing isn't something we're meant to do alone, though trauma often isolates us. A support system—whether it's friends, family, or a professional network—can provide the emotional and practical resources you need as you navigate your journey.

1. Identifying Safe and Supportive People

Start by taking stock of the people in your life who have shown you care and kindness. Who makes you feel safe? Who listens without judgment? Building a support system means surrounding yourself with people who respect your boundaries and can offer you a non-judgmental space to heal.

It's okay if your circle is small at first. It's better to have a few genuinely supportive individuals than a large number of acquaintances who don't really "get" what you're going through.

2. Reaching Out for Help

One of the hardest parts of healing is asking for help. Trauma often teaches us to keep everything to ourselves, but healing thrives in connection. When you feel ready, reach out to those you trust. Share a bit of your experience, even if it's hard. It doesn't have to be a deep conversation right away; just letting someone know that you're going through a tough time can be a relief.

When I first started reaching out for support, I realized how many people around me had gone through similar struggles. Sharing your story, even in small doses, opens up space for empathy and connection. You don't have to do it alone.

3. Creating a Healing Network

In addition to your personal support system, consider building a broader healing network. This might include joining a trauma support group, working with a therapist, or engaging in online communities focused on recovery. Finding others who understand your journey can be incredibly validating.

I once joined a trauma recovery group, and I remember how comforting it was to be surrounded by people who "got it." There's something healing about hearing others' stories and realizing you're not alone.

Reclaiming your sense of safety and control is a gradual process, but every step you take is a step toward healing. Learning to feel safe in your body, re-establishing control through daily routines, and building a supportive environment all contribute to a stronger foundation for recovery.

Healing is not about rushing through the process—it's about being gentle with yourself, celebrating small victories, and trusting that with time, you'll begin to feel safer, more grounded, and more in control of your life. You're building your way back to yourself, and every bit of progress counts.

Conclusion

Healing from trauma does not happen in a day. It's a whole journey—sometimes filled with breakthroughs, and other times with setbacks. But every step you take, no matter how small, is progress. You're not simply moving away from the pain, you're moving toward reclaiming your life, your sense of self, and your well-being.

Throughout this book, we've discussed various ways to reconnect with your body, mind, and spirit, and how each approach—whether it's through relational therapy, somatic practices, or cognitive behavioral techniques—can support you on your healing journey. More than anything, I hope you see that you are not alone in this process. Trauma might make you feel isolated, but the truth is, there is a community of survivors, healers, and professionals who understand and are here to help.

One of the key things to remember is that healing takes time and that's okay. There's no rush. Some days you'll feel stronger, and other days the weight of what you've been through will feel heavy. On those days, give yourself grace.

If there's one thing I'd like to leave you with, it's this: you have the power to heal. Trauma may have shaped parts of your life, but it does not define you. You are resilient, you are capable, and you have the strength to rebuild your life.

Thank You for Reading!

Thank you so much for choosing to read my book. It means the world to me that you've taken the time to engage with my work.

I poured my heart and soul into creating this book, spending countless hours to ensure it would be something truly valuable for you. Now that you've read it, I'd love to hear your thoughts.

If you found this book helpful or inspiring, would you mind leaving a review? Your honest feedback not only helps me grow as a writer but also supports other readers in discovering my work. Each review makes a big difference, especially for independent authors like me.

I deeply appreciate your time and support. Knowing that my words have reached and resonated with you is the best reward I could ask for.

Thank you again, and I look forward to hearing from you.

Laura Gardner Publishing

Like this one, I have many other books with amazing titles that you will want to read. Scan the code below to find them now!